Chloe Smith is a mum of three, who suffered from extreme depression and anxiety. With always sensing things to happen before they happen and being open to the spiritual world, it was not until her nan past she had her spiritual awakening, with sensing everyone's emotions and feelings by looking at them, to your past loved ones, ghosts and angels surrounding you, she now deliver messages globally, helping you with obstacles in life. She can focus on just a photo of yourself to read for you!

I dedicate this book to my parents, Dean and Emma, for supporting my weirdness growing up.

My partner, Mason, and our children, George, Charlie and Ivy for continuous support. But also, my nan, Susan. For giving me my spiritual awakening, forever chasing rainbows.

Chloe Smith

LIFE OF A PSYCHIC/MEDIUM

AUSTIN MACAULEY PUBLISHERS™
LONDON · CAMBRIDGE · NEW YORK · SHARJAH

Copyright © Chloe Smith 2024

The right of Chloe Smith to be identified as author of this work has been asserted by the author in accordance with sections 77 and 78 of the Copyright, Designs and Patents Act 1988.

All rights reserved. No part of this publication may be reproduced, stored in a retrieval system, or transmitted in any form or by any means, electronic, mechanical, photocopying, recording, or otherwise, without the prior permission of the publishers.

Any person who commits any unauthorised act in relation to this publication may be liable to criminal prosecution and civil claims for damages.

A CIP catalogue record for this title is available from the British Library.

ISBN 9781035837175 (Paperback)
ISBN 9781035837182 (Hardback)
ISBN 9781035837199 (ePub e-book)

www.austinmacauley.co.uk

First Published 2024
Austin Macauley Publishers Ltd®
1 Canada Square
Canary Wharf
London
E14 5AA

Table of Contents

Introduction	9
Chapter 1: Do You Believe in The Afterlife?	12
Chapter 2: We Are Protected, But How? Angels Of Course	14
Chapter 3: Rules	18
Chapter 4: Spiritual Awakening	22
Chapter 5: Meditation	29
Chapter 6: Auras and Chakras	32
Chapter 7: Crystals	39
Chapter 8: Anxiety and Depression	42
Chapter 9: The Power of The Moon	44
Chapter 10: Tarot Cards	48
Chapter 11: Manifestation	52
Energy Exercises	55
Often Asked Questions	57

Introduction

It seems surreal, doesn't it? How can someone talk to the dead? Well, here I am writing a book on just that. Seeing, hearing and sensing Ghosts, Spirits and Angels were all a part of my life from very early on. Though for many years I didn't understand them, or even acknowledge them. I had an idyllic childhood and was blessed with a caring family. But I always felt different somehow. Perhaps the sensitivity to spirit around me and strange dreams. Sensing things to happen before they were about too were one of the main things I noticed, that feeling stayed with me until I reached my mid—20s—As cliché as it may sound, I finally found my true self.

Over the years my psychic side came more prevalent and began to feel drawn to sensing people's feelings, the joy, the fear, and the pain. Even though this is difficult sometimes; I am also able to see their potential, which is inspiring. I learnt that all these feelings explain my caring nature and its only now I understand my full intuition is true and very real. I have worked with some outstanding spirit guides who have patiently helped me along the way. This book will be fulfilled with facts, true moments and how you could be just like me. Have you often questioned a lot about life? Or even felt you didn't fit in? Well, I promise you will enjoy reading this book just as much as I did writing it.

I never felt like I succeeded well with life's challenges other than my own children. I have three beautiful children, all close in age. Although I would not change it for the world, I certainly struggled along the way. Being a parent Is tough! I cried many days, counting down the hours until bedtime. This is where my depression and anxiety grew, I felt trapped. I could not leave the house, my partner Mason, worked long hours building his business, my parents lived in France, I didn't not have the support network I desperately craved. For this time period I shut off all my spirituality, it was not until my nan passed, I had a light bulb moment. I was closer to her than anyone and sadly she got sick and passed over. I remember texting my mom the exact time she took her last breath. I went to her funeral and there she was, glowing, in the corner of the room. I thought it was my mind playing tricks on me, but she appeared in the car, my house and everything became stronger! This is when I noticed Charlotte in my house, The Victorian girl who plays with George, it sounds strange I know! But she's harmless, she passes me on the stairs daily. And sits by my feet when I watch telly. Charlotte is a Ghost, which means she is tied to the location of her death, I could send her to the light. But she is safe and at peace here, after all its her home.

So here I am on my journey, I found myself with definite purpose. I want to share my acquired knowledge and understandings with an audience to help you open to your spiritual and psychic development. I don't consider myself to be special, I have simply chosen to pursue this avenue, to open and connect with the Universe and to develop my own natural abilities.

Love Chloe x

Chapter 1
Do You Believe in The Afterlife?

No matter your background or beliefs, I believe anyone is capable of connecting with the spirit world. Firstly, it's very important what your intentions are in why you would like to connect – maybe wanting to make sure your loved one is happy and at peace? Or want to share and receive messages of love. Everyone's reasons might be different. And that is fine.

But my first question is: Do you believe in the afterlife? If you have strong doubts, you will block your ability to connect with loved ones. It's okay to have these moments where you question what happens. But if you are completely answering this question as a no, then it's hard to believe your loved ones are there. Most people have doubts because they are afraid.

If you start talking about spirit guides and the afterlife, you're almost scared of people's reactions. The world we live in today emphasises science and proof. But if we sit back and disconnect from the world—TV and radios—then what does your heart tell you? Where are your departed loved ones? Do you believe they're still with you? Bodies might be far away, but their loving energy still surrounds us. Believing in the spirit world helps us come to terms with the void in our lives.

When you die, your soul leaves your physical body, and all pain and suffering disappear. You are reunited with your past loved ones, guides, and pets, and it's a place of happiness and light. I know it may sound hard to believe, especially if you don't see your loved ones straight away, but start trusting yourself. You are more than capable of opening your heart and mind to the spiritual world.

We all have powers of intuition. Most people don't use it, or simply don't know how. But in fact, it's one of the most magical and wonderful gifts. It mainly comes from the gut and your emotional centre, rather than your head. Come on, we've all been there – how many times have you had that gut feeling about something and not listened to it? Then think to yourself, 'I knew that would happen.' This is precisely what I'm talking about. Once you begin trusting your intuition, one of the many obstacles to connecting with spirits will be lifted. It may not be so easy – especially if your intuition is telling you something you don't want to know. But I'm here to tell you that it will protect and guide you. Logic can often provide misguided advice, so it's crucial to learn to open up to intuition. If this starts to worry you and you begin to experience a lot of fear or even questions about your intuition, then I find meditation very helpful in creating a calm state of mind. But while you're connected with your intuition, the spirits will be very close to you.

Chapter 2
We Are Protected, But How?
Angels Of Course

Throughout our life here on Earth, we have protectors. Our past loved ones will come down to earth and support us through life's challenges, but how is that possible? Of course, we will question what happens when we die, but everything around us is surrounded by energy and vibrations. There is the physical plane, the Astral plane, the Causal Plane. Even though this can sound confusing, it is very similar to the stages of a human: Infant, Child, Adult, Death. The way to communicate with spirit is all about movement. I must move myself to a higher level to communicate. We are at the bottom, spirit is at the top, and we meet in the middle (mediumship).

Spirit can go here, there, and everywhere, surrounding us when we are feeling sad or happy. Although I am not sure if you sit around in coffee shops in the spirit world, I do know there is life after death. Else, how would I be able to communicate with the dead? Do I look different to spirit? Why do they channel me? I often ask myself this, but I would not change it for the world. I get an overwhelming feeling of love and peace when I make a connection. And with Angels,

I also feel protected. Angels give us unconditional love. No matter if we make mistakes in life, they are still there.

We all have at least one Angel who will be there our entire lives, offering guidance through moments of darkness, helping point you in the right direction. We also have a few other angels that have important roles.

Protector Angel: With us closely through our spiritual and psychic development.

Healer Angel: Inspiring us to look after ourselves better, getting fitter and healthier. Giving us healing energy.

Message bearer: Amplifying our intuitive messages, helping our intuition and gut feelings.

Helper Angel: Helping us with development on a particular skill/project.

It makes me laugh, really. If I lose something, I ask for my Angel to help me. And it will appear. You should try it. It really will surprise you. Angels don't have names. However, our amazing minds work well with shape and form, helping us identify them and focus our energies, making a better connection with them.

It's incredible how they'll present themselves. Some people see their Angels very vividly and in full detail. While others see shadow figures or in our minds, we can focus on what they will look like. This is fine. However, they come as a blessing either way. Most people do name their angels. It helps you connect and tune in with their energy. A name usually comes strongly to your mind. My guardian Angel is called Skyla. Some people don't get a name straight to their mind, so when trying to connect, simply ask, "may I call you?" and assign them a name. The important thing to know is that guides may not show you their shadow or full detail in the way you're hoping and could appear in dreams, bring messages and ideas directly to your mind, or assist you to feel 'urges which will guide you one way or another on the spiritual or physical path. You could even have a prominent animal guide who acts as a companion. Even through number sequences like 111, or you might have a lucky number. You could be attending a job interview, and the number is in the company address. Sometimes you just must listen, and you will understand them. Little signs are real. Rather amazing if you ask me. Your guardian angels know you, and so they know which signs will capture your awareness, and what items contain personal meaning and significance for you. They can then use these things to help guide your next steps. Don't forget, if you are looking for some guidance, just ask your Angel for a sign. When you notice a sign that may be from an angel… Breathe, be aware, and thank your angels for reaching out with their love and guidance. Let's go through some signs you may notice and what they mean.

Feathers:

Feathers are a popular sign from your angels. They are a beautiful reminder that your angels are near, loving, and supporting you from behind the scenes. When you find feathers in a place that is somewhat abnormal, it is an especially powerful angelic sign. Sometimes I'll step right outside my door, and there is a feather.

Flickering lights:

Angelic energy is powerful! And when you're in the presence of angels, the actual lighting around you may show signs of this increase in energy. It is actually an easier way for your loved ones and angels to communicate through electricity. This angel sign could take the form of the lights around you, like a lamp in your room, flickering. It may also take the form of a light turning itself on with no clear reason for why that should have happened.

Angel Numbers:

One of the most common ways angels will attempt to capture your attention and guide you is through angel numbers. Whether you are sitting in traffic behind a car with 333 on the licence plate or you seem to look over at the clock at just the right time, like 11:11 exactly, angel numbers have specific meanings for you. But it's a way for your guides and angels to get your attention.

000 – A new beginning is near.
111 – You're on the correct path.
222 – Keep having faith; trust yourself.
333 – Embrace creativity and growth.
444 – Prepare for the guidance of angels.
555 – Change is imminent; be hopeful.
666 – Refocus and pay closer attention.
777 – Look for direct divine guidance.
888 – You're on a path to financial success.
999 – Turn negativity into positivity.

Chapter 3
Rules

There are many important rules to follow while connecting with the spirit world. It is normal to feel anxious, but remaining calm and maintaining a positive mindset is crucial. In this discussion, I will focus on communicating with spirits. However, I understand that some individuals may have concerns about this.

It is essential to note that spirits should never harm you or encourage any harmful actions towards yourself or others. If you ever feel uneasy or concerned, seek assistance from an experienced and reputable medium or healer. While it is important to take this process seriously, it can also be enjoyable, and laughter can raise the vibrational energy.

Discovering your preferred method of relaxation is also a valuable tip. The more you can disconnect from external distractions, the easier it becomes to establish a connection. It is natural to occasionally feel confused or have your mind wander, but keeping a journal can be helpful. By documenting the exercises you perform and taking notes on your meditation experiences, you can look back and gain a better understanding of your progress. This practice has personally helped me learn a great deal.

Every morning upon waking, I always ask for protection. I also do this before engaging in any psychic or spiritual development work. Even if you ever feel uneasy, it brings peace of mind to request the presence of your Spirit Guides, Angels, and loved ones in spirit to draw close and keep you safe and protected. Closing your eyes while seeking protection can aid in maintaining a sense of calm.

How to ask for protection:

1. Concentrate on your breathing, allowing your breath to become slower and deeper. Give it a try now: Take a deep breath through your nose and exhale through your mouth. Repeat this process three times. It helps you relax, and you can feel your thoughts drifting away as your feelings and intuition begin to take over.
2. You can say the following out loud or in your mind:

"I call upon my Spirit Guides, Angels, and loved ones in spirit to draw close to me and create a circle of protection around me, ensuring my safety. I invite you to share your messages of love. I wish for no negative spirits to enter."

Now that you are protected and all set to begin your spiritual journey, I would like to introduce you to a grounding technique. This technique is fantastic, and you're going to love it! Whenever I feel tired or unbalanced, this is my go-to exercise. Grounding is all about visualisation. Below, I will provide a step-by-step guide on how I ground myself. Keep in mind that many people use different techniques, so go with whatever comes to your mind instantly!

Grounding:

1. Sit in a comfortable and relaxed position. Begin by closing your eyes.
2. Focus on your breathing.
3. Visualise that you have thick roots, similar to the roots of a tree. Picture these roots growing from the soles of your feet, extending down through the floor, and reaching deep into the ground towards the centre core of the earth. Imagine a bright star, radiating warmth and light. Envision your roots wrapping around this star. As the glowing energy from the star reaches your roots, imagine it flowing up through your body, filling you with warmth, light, energy, and a sense of vitality. Feel this energy expanding and shining from the crown of your head.

As you practise grounding properly, you may start to experience a tingling sensation in your feet, similar to pins and needles. Grounding helps you stay connected to the physical world while your spirit explores different planes of existence. By grounding yourself, you will feel more anchored and protected.

In my daily communication with spirit, I have developed various techniques to avoid feeling drained by energies. One of my most effective techniques is what I call the "Chloe bubble." Whenever I feel anxious, exhausted, or struggle with sleep, I visualise placing myself inside a protective bubble. This bubble acts as a shield, preventing anyone or anything from disturbing me, and I can pop it whenever I choose. This technique helps me feel safe and relaxed. You can also create bubbles around other people if needed. For instance, I find supermarkets challenging due to the high volume of people. I can sense their emotions and feelings, which can be draining. Creating a bubble helps me maintain my energetic boundaries.

Visualisation is truly amazing. It allows us to create mental images and transport ourselves to any desired location simply by closing our eyes. Whether it's imagining being on a beach or connecting with departed loved ones, the power of the human mind is remarkable. Our minds consist of a constant flow of thoughts, feelings, memories, and sensations. Although we all have a voice in our heads that sounds like us and knows a lot about us, it's important to recognize that this voice is not our true essence. It's a part of our mind. As human beings, we often fear negative experiences such as illness, aging, and death. However, there is life after death, and we are reunited with our past loved ones. I know this because I have witnessed loved ones coming to guide their relatives before they pass away. They are waiting to greet them on the other side.

Chapter 4
Spiritual Awakening

I had extreme nightmares growing up and felt like I didn't fit in with the world, and although I could always sense when things would happen, I didn't really use my abilities until my nan passed away. This is called a 'spiritual awakening'! A spiritual awakening is a call to higher consciousness and deeper mental awareness.

For many, a spiritual awakening is brought about by a life – changing event: The death of a loved one, divorce, and more. For others, it is a gradual and subtle shift. Because life was difficult and I was going through a lot of my own challenges with being a full-time parent, managing anxiety and depression, it was only until my nan passed that I was able to awaken my spiritual self to the full extent. It was my life's plan, and it makes sense to me why my passion for other hobbies never lasted. I was once a dog groomer, a craft maker, and even a photographer, but my passion soon faded, and this is the reason why. Even though I could have skipped straight to spirituality, which was always a part of me, I still needed to have these other experiences to make me who I am today.

Whether you were triggered by an event in your life and found your spiritual path, or you have simply chosen this avenue to go down, I believe it's for a reason we have been brought together today. As you go through a spiritual awakening, you may feel a variety of symptoms from time to time. You may feel an increase of your intuition and sense of awareness. 'Lucid Dreams' – These are dreams in which you know you are dreaming or feel as if you are awake within the dream. Sounds a little crazy, but it's rather peaceful.

If you have psychic abilities, it does not necessarily mean you are a medium. The most important difference between a psychic and a medium is that psychics do not communicate with spirits, whereas mediums do. Mediums talk to the dead; they communicate with those who have passed on from this world. You may just know something about someone without them telling you, or you may sense that something is going to happen before it happens. But how do we become a psychic medium? Recognition is your first step. Even though I have been a Psychic/Medium my whole life, it is still something I often ask myself: 'Do I look different to spirit? Do they know I can communicate with them?' It sounds a little bonkers that I can communicate with the dead. Sometimes I can have a full conversation with past loved ones, or I get shown messages and signs. They even use my body as a channel. But of course, we get some sceptics who don't believe in the existence of a spirit world, and that's fine also – but we all have spiritual abilities, but many of us avoid the fact or don't open our hearts and minds to the messages that surround us on a day-to-day basis. The truth is, anyone is capable of communicating with the other side, but you need to trust in the wisdom you receive. You may receive messages in different ways, so it's a time for you to learn which is the way you get your messages.

1. Clairaudient – **Clear Hearing**

You will hear spirit either audibly or inside your head, almost like it's your own voice. For you, you may hear an actual name or a suggestion of a name. You can hear spirit.

2. Clairvoyance – **Clear Seeing**

You may see things physically, or you may just see images in your head, almost like a movie playing in your mind. So, you may see a symbol or image of their name. You know the past and the future.

3. Claircognizance – **Clear Knowing**

You just have to know about things. For you, you may have a 'knowing' of their name. The answers just come to you.

4. Clairsentient – **Clear Feeling**

These are the feelers, the empaths. People who have this feel their angel's guidance in their bodies and in their heart. So you may feel the vibration of their name or what their name means. They use your body as a channel.

5. Clairalience – Clear Smelling

This is being able to smell odours that don't have any kind of physical source. Instances of this could include smelling the perfume or the cigarette smoke of a deceased relative. When our sense of smell is strong and distinct, we may find that certain smells connect us to past memories, or we may be drawn to working as a florist, a wine taster, or a perfume fragrance creator.

Like radio waves, spiritual information is constantly being broadcast around us, so it's just a matter of learning how to tune in to it. The Clair senses are types of psychic abilities that correspond with the senses of seeing, hearing, feeling, and smelling. When I tap into my intuition and spirit energy, my mind and body become flooded with mental impressions: thoughts, feelings, images, sounds, tastes, and smells. It's about raising your vibration up as the spirits slow theirs down, and you meet in the middle so you can receive these messages. So, relax.

Spirit has different ways of communicating with us through these senses but also through other means:

Dreams: Our minds and bodies are so much at peace when we sleep; it's the easiest way for any messages to come forward. You will remember what is important for you to remember, and your loved ones will come forward, especially in the beginning of their passing. They're usually just trying to show you that they're safe and at peace.

Fragrance: You might experience a sudden waft of the person's perfume, smoke, or the smell of their favourite foods or flowers.

Music: When you hear your deceased loved one's favourite song, they are reaching out to you through the music. If you're listening to the radio or walking into a store and their song comes on, it's a sign that they are with you and want you to remember how much they love you. You might also get the song stuck in your head or notice yourself humming it out of the blue.

Orbs: Advancement of technology has allowed photography to capture balls of electrical energy. Orbs are believed to be spirits. If you take a photograph and notice circular balls of energy around you, this is a sign your loved one is present.

Rainbow: Seeing a rainbow at a funeral or shortly after one is a sign that your loved one's spirit **has reached** its next destination. It signifies peace and the presence of their spirit.

Butterflies: Butterflies are often seen as representations of the human soul in many cultures. They symbolise endurance, hope, and the cycle of life. Their presence can be interpreted as a sign from the spiritual realm, reminding us of the transformative power of the soul and the beauty of life's journey.

Birds: Feathers are commonly seen as a sign from departed loved ones, but certain types of birds can also carry symbolic meaning. For example, if you spot a hummingbird near your home, especially if they are not typically seen in your area, shortly after the passing of a loved one, it can be interpreted as a sign or message from the spirit world. The appearance of a hummingbird in such circumstances may be seen as a meaningful connection or presence of your departed loved one.

As your mediumship abilities develop, you will start to recognize the unique ways in which you receive messages. For instance, some mediums may sense the presence of a spirit on a specific side, either to represent the maternal or paternal lineage, either in relation to themselves or the person they are reading for. It will require trial and error to understand and interpret these nuances.

It can be challenging to comprehend the distinctions between spirits, ghosts, and angels, as they each occupy different realms of existence. Angels exist on a higher plane of consciousness, whereas ghosts are tied to the location of their death. Ghosts and paranormal activity are often more commonly discussed because they are the first encounters people have with the spirit world while remaining connected to the earthly plane. When we pass away, our soul separates from the physical body, and any pain or suffering dissipates. Our spirit continues to exist beyond death, but in some cases, a spirit may remain tied to the earthly realm for various reasons. This could be due to a strong attachment to their home or a traumatic or sudden death. Occasionally, a ghostly presence may be a reenactment of past energy or a time lapse, where the energy of a past event is replayed. I have personally experienced instances where I have been startled by such ghostly encounters, although it is important to note that they typically do not intend to frighten but rather reflect an energetic imprint of their past.

Chapter 5
Meditation

Meditation, in its simplest form, aims to bring about a sense of calmness, relaxation, and reconnection with past loved ones, spirit guides, and angels. It can be as easy as directing your attention to your breath or using a candle flame as a focal point. Regardless of the technique you choose, meditation is a profoundly effective way to enhance your spiritual development. Through meditation, we enter an altered state of consciousness. I recommend that during meditation, you mentally return to your starting point or have a keyword or phrase that can bring you back to wakefulness if needed. This way, you remain in a state of awareness while also being deeply relaxed. Isn't it fantastic?

To meditate effectively, it's important to find a quiet and distraction-free space. It's difficult to relax if you're constantly aware of external noises or tasks that need your attention. Choose a position that feels comfortable for you and begin by entering a relaxation phase. This initial relaxation helps you unwind before diving into the meditation practice.

Focusing on your breath becomes the anchor that allows your body to relax and your mind to clear. As you meditate, thoughts and images may naturally arise and fade away. It's impossible to completely empty your mind, but when distractions arise, simply refocus on your breath to bring your attention back to the present moment.

1) Are you comfortable? Try sitting with your hands on your knees, and your palms facing upwards. Take your awareness to your breathing.
2) During this meditation, you are calm and protected. If you wish to come out of meditation, you can do so at any time by counting from 3 to 1.
3) Take a slow, deep breath in for a count of three, hold the breath for two, and then exhale slowly for another count of three. If your mind starts to wander, refocus on your breathing and count again.

Once you are in this relaxed state of mind, you will begin to perceive images that are not related to your own thoughts and daily activities. You may receive words, ideas, or even messages from loved ones. It's also possible to see different colours during your meditation. It is common to doubt and think that you're making these things up afterward, but I encourage you to write down anything you remember. Over time, it will start to make sense to you or someone close to you. You will learn to differentiate between your own thoughts and messages from the spirit.

Try this technique and see where it takes you:

1. Light a white candle, sit down, close your eyes and take a deep breath. Say you that you'd like to communicate with your loved ones and guides and ask them a question, take a deep breath and relax, and relax your hand. Let it be loose, and then write up that they're saying. You may hear spirit or messages will come directly to your mind. They'll start talking fast. Trust yourself and the process.

Chapter 6
Auras and Chakras

Life is composed of energy, and everything around us possesses energy. Understanding the concepts of Auras and Chakras can be compared to a science class. Allow me to explain to the best of my ability. Developing our spiritual skills requires us to grasp some understanding of energy theories.

Let's start with Auras. Our physical body is primarily made up of millions of cells, each vibrating at a slow rate and emitting a certain amount of energy. Surrounding this physical body is a lighter and finer energy body that vibrates at a higher rate than our cells. This energy field is what we call the Aura. The Aura can be described as a field of energy or light that envelops every physical body on Earth. Each individual has their own Aura, which exhibits various spiritual colours. These colours of the Aura can vary depending on the current state of the Aura. It is worth noting that Auras can reveal imbalances or indications of poor health in an individual, but I prefer to focus on positivity and guidance rather than solely on identifying health issues. Nevertheless, it remains fascinating. The Aura can be considered a "mirror" that reflects our present mental, physical, and spiritual state. With practice and experience, it is possible to tune into someone's Aura and gather information from it, either visually or through a sense of knowing or feeling. Many people believe that when we instantaneously develop a dislike towards a person or place, it is because the energy of our Auras is not compatible for some reason.

Chakras

Within our Auras, there is a central vertical column aligned with our spine, which houses our chakras. Like Auras, Chakras are associated with specific spiritual colours. The term "Chakra" originates from Sanskrit and refers to spinning vortexes of energy. These energy centres are located within our physical bodies. There are seven main Chakras, each connected to a major organ. These Chakras serve as "power stations" responsible for distributing energy throughout the body. Although each Chakra contains all colour vibrations, one particular colour dominates each Chakra. When perceiving colours, trust your intuition. I understand that it may seem challenging to grasp these concepts, but with time and practice, you will develop a better understanding. Trust yourself more. There are also smaller Chakras, such as those in the palms of our hands, which are used for healing and Reiki, as well as the soles of our feet, which are associated with grounding techniques.

It is essential to keep your Chakras open. When they become blocked, you may experience physical or emotional symptoms related to a specific Chakra. For instance, feelings of insecurity, loneliness, and greed, or physical issues such as headaches, indigestion, and colon problems. To ensure that your Chakras remain unblocked, it is beneficial to allocate time for yourself, spend time in nature, focus on your breath, and engage in other cleansing practices.

Now that we have a better understanding of Chakras and Auras, let's delve into the meaning of colours. If we observe our daily lives, we will notice that we often associate colours with various expressions and emotions. For example, we associate red with anger and feeling blue with sadness. We paint rooms with bright colours to create a bright and cheerful environment. Colours play a significant role in setting the mood and atmosphere.

Here is a breakdown of the spiritual colours associated with each Chakra:

Root Chakra – RED: Located at the base of the spine, the root chakra provides a foundation for life, grounding us and instilling a sense of security and stability. Red is an intense and passionate aura colour, associated with the root chakra that develops in the first seven years of our lives. It represents the physical plane, grounding, security, and instinct.

Sacral Chakra – ORANGE: Located above the pubic bone and below the navel, the sacral chakra is all about emotions, passions, and pleasures. It represents our emotional satisfaction and brings us joy. An imbalance in this chakra may result in withdrawal from sensual signals and a need to express our emotions and feelings more. People with orange auras are often adventure seekers, exhibiting passionate and creative energy. Use the colour orange to uplift your spirits and boost your confidence.

Solar Plexus Chakra – YELLOW: Positioned from the navel to the ribcage, the solar plexus chakra is associated with metabolic and digestive functions. An overly open solar plexus chakra may make us susceptible to external energies, requiring us to learn self-protection. Yellow auras symbolise creativity, intelligence, and an unwavering desire to seek out fun experiences. Those with yellow auras have a mood that is nearly impossible to bring down.

Heart Chakra – GREEN (can also be pink): Situated in the centre of the chest, the heart chakra encompasses the heart, thymus gland, lungs, and breasts. It represents unconditional love and connects us to the spiritual aspect of ourselves and others. Individuals with intense green in their auras are typically drawn to nature and animals and possess a natural ability for self-healing.

Throat Chakra – BLUE: Located in the throat, this chakra is associated with expression. It governs the thyroid, parathyroid, jaw, neck, mouth, tongue, and larynx. An open throat chakra enables us to listen attentively, speak clearly, and express ourselves effectively. If you are drawn to the colour blue or have a blue aura, you may be emotionally sensitive and self-expressive. It is important to listen when individuals with teal auras speak, as they may be shy in sharing their innermost feelings. Those with teal auras tend to be empathic and sensitive.

Third Eye or Brow Chakra – INDIGO OR VIOLET: Positioned between the eyebrows, the third eye chakra governs the pituitary gland, eyes, head, and lower part of the brain. It serves as a bridge between our inner selves and the outside world, allowing us to see through illusions and perceive the clear picture. This chakra is associated with psychic perception, intuition, sensitivity, strength, and spirituality. If you resonate with indigo or violet colours, you are on the right path.

Crown Chakra – VIOLET OR WHITE: Located at the crown of the head, the crown chakra represents enlightenment and our spiritual connection to our higher selves and the universe. It connects us to the spiritual plane and embodies purity, authority, peace, and goodness. The crown chakra is associated with the colour violet, which links everyone to the energy of the universe.

You can also cleanse your Aura to ensure you are purified and refreshed. There are various methods to achieve this. If you feel that you are carrying negative energy due to emotional experiences or environmental factors, it may impact your mind, body, and soul in some way.

Cleansing your Aura:

1) **Walk in the rain** – Rainwater is the water at its purest form. Walking while it's raining and imagining your negative energies getting washed off with water droplets can really help you neutralise your energy. And you can even cleanse crystals this way too!
2) **Take a Salt Bath** – Sea salt is considered the best natural cleansing agent. It has the ability to drain away negative energies and magically cleanse and purify your aura.

3) **Reiki** – An energy healer has the ability to read and analyse your aura, and they can also assist you in cleansing it.
4) **Friendships** – The people you choose to surround yourself with can significantly influence your aura. It is beneficial to be around individuals who have an optimistic and supportive outlook on life.

Third eye:

You may have heard of the Third Eye, which is considered to be the spiritual eye connecting us to the spiritual realm. It is not a physical object but a metaphorical opening that can be visualised in the middle of the forehead, between the brows. The Third Eye is associated with clairvoyance and is used to develop spiritual abilities and establish a connection with the spirit world. Opening and activating the Third Eye can enhance intuition, access the subconscious mind, and provide guidance.

Here's a simple exercise to engage your Third Eye:

1. Find a quiet and comfortable place to sit or lie down.
2. Close your eyes and focus your attention on the point between your eyebrows.
3. Visualise a tunnel of golden light in that area.
4. Mentally enter the tunnel and allow yourself to be enveloped in a sense of happiness and freedom.
5. As you move through the tunnel, imagine the light bathing you, and let go of all thoughts and distractions.

6. By practising this exercise, you can stimulate and activate your Third Eye, allowing for a deeper connection to your intuition and spiritual insights.

Chapter 7
Crystals

How can a crystal heal you? I often asked myself this question when I suffered from extreme headaches, stress, and anxiety. I was willing to try anything, so I purchased an Amethyst Crystal, and to my amazement, my headache vanished. Now, I wear an Amethyst necklace daily, and it works wonders for me. There are over a hundred different crystals, each with different properties depending on their energy. Crystals can be used for healing, protection, meditation, manifesting, and much more.

Crystals start small and grow as more atoms are added. They can grow from water rich in dissolved minerals, melted rock, and even vapour. When something is wrong in our lives, whether it's physical, mental, emotional, or spiritual, it's often because our own energy vibration isn't quite right. By carrying the right crystal or placing it in our energy field, our energy vibration can be corrected. Isn't that fantastic? This is how crystals helped alleviate my headaches. However, please remember that if you suspect you have a medical problem, it's important to seek professional advice.

So, how do you know which crystal you need? Find a place that sells crystals and see which one you are most drawn to. Let the crystal pick you! Once you choose your crystal, you might find it warm or as though it has a pulse, connecting with you.

I would recommend cleansing a new crystal when you purchase it. The reason for this is that someone else could have handled the crystal and left their energy behind. Cleansing can be done in many ways, such as leaving your crystal in direct sunlight for a few hours, placing it under the light of a full moon, holding it in a flowing stream in nature, or rinsing it under a tap. Ask for all negativity to go away. Remember to recharge your crystals regularly. Below, I will list three crystals that I use regularly.

1) **Amethyst – Purple:** Known for spiritual healing, calmness, and wisdom. Provides stress, anxiety, and headache relief. It helps reduce negative energy and awakens your third eye.
2) **Clear Quartz:** Enhances mental clarity. It can help with emotional stability and is popular in mediation and restorative work. It's also often used for manifestation and can help create more focus and clarity around desires. It is a protective stone that can be used to amplify psychic abilities.
3) **Carnelian – Orange:** Restores vitality and motivation, stimulates creativity. Gives courage, promotes positive life choices, dispels apathy, and motivates for success.

Clear Quartz Test:

1. Take two cups of tap water.
2. Put a clear quartz into one of the cups of water and leave it for at least 10 minutes.
3. Remove the quartz and taste both cups of water. Can you taste a difference?

Clear Quartz is an excellent purifying crystal that can alter the taste of tap water!

Chapter 8
Anxiety and Depression

A subject close to my heart, but I do believe we all go through anxiety and depression throughout our lives. After all, life is tough and challenging. Being more open to the spiritual world has helped me, and I believe it will help you too. Anxiety is the feeling of being tense, nervous, or unable to relax. It includes having a sense of dread or fearing the worst, feeling like the world is speeding up or slowing down. Depression can be linked to feeling sad, down, and lacking motivation. If you have followed my journey as Chloe Mediumship, you will know that I was on the maximum dosage of antidepressants anyone could take. However, I am not on them anymore. Thanks to believing in myself and embracing the world from nature to spirit, I have become a stronger, independent person. And so can you.

Try staying active as a good way to keep your mind and body clear. Use stress management and relaxation techniques. Remember, it is okay to have bad days. But write down your emotions and feelings. It will help you feel less bottled up and provide a release point. You can even connect with your past loved ones and angels through writing and drawing. Let's try an exercise.

1. Calm your mind and relax your body. Focus on your breathing, ensuring it is slow and deep.
2. Ask your loved ones to step forward.
3. Ask for a physical sign to know your guides are around. Be patient and relax.
4. Make a mental note of anything you feel around you, such as a gentle touch, change in energy, heat, or cold.
5. Once you feel a sensation, ask them to show you again.

- **The Solar Plexus Chakra** is related to anxiety. This chakra regulates our fears, sense of power, and gut feelings. When this chakra is out of balance, we experience fears, eating disorders, anxiety, and a loss of control. To balance this chakra:
- Try new things.
- Spend time in the sun.
- Practice yoga for the Solar Plexus Chakra.
- Meditate.

Chapter 9
The Power of The Moon

The Moon is indeed very powerful and represents powerful feminine energy, while the Sun is known as male energy. It symbolises wisdom, intuition, and a spiritual connection. The Moon moves through different cycles and does not remain fixed, symbolising the cycle of life itself. After all, in life, we often find ourselves in different phases throughout our lives.

1) **New Moon** – The Moon can't be seen from Earth as it's in between the Earth and the Sun. This phase is associated with new beginnings. You may experience moodiness or tiredness during a full moon.
2) **Waxing Crescent Moon** – The Moon's illumination is growing, but we can only see less than half of the Moon from Earth. This phase is linked to making inventions and resolutions.
3) **First Quarter Moon** – Half of the Moon is in shadow.
4) **Waxing Gibbous Moon** – A gibbous Moon is when we can see over half of it illuminated. A waxing gibbous Moon means it is getting brighter. This phase is associated with practice and refinement.

5) **Full Moon** – A full moon means the Sun is illuminating the whole Moon. It appears as a bright circle in the sky. This phase is associated with setting intentions and releasing things that do not serve us. You can leave your crystals outside; the power of the Moon will recharge them.
6) **Waning Gibbous Moon** – We already know that gibbous means that more than half of the Moon is illuminated. However, when it wanders, it means the brightness of the Moon is decreasing. This phase is associated with gratitude and giving thanks.
7) **Third Quarter** – We can see only half of the Moon, but it's the opposite side of what we saw in the first quarter. This phase is associated with forgiveness.
8) **Waning Crescent Moon** – The Moon's brightness is dimming. We can see less than a quarter of the Moon. This phase is associated with surrender.

The Moon is indeed fascinating, and it is known to be linked to fertility and childbirth. There tends to be more births during the full moon than at any other time in the lunar cycle.

Now, what exactly is a lunar cycle? It is the representation of the Moon's journey around the Earth. As I mentioned earlier, the Moon moves between the Earth and the Sun, creating a shadow on the far side of the Moon, which limits the light that is reflected to Earth. It may sound confusing at first, but as you develop a connection with the Moon, you will gradually understand and feel drawn to learn more.

This is where Zodiac signs come into play. A sign of the zodiac refers to one of the 12 constellations of the zodiac that the Sun passes through. A person's particular zodiac sign is determined by the constellation the Sun was in at the time of their birth. These zodiac signs can provide insights into a person's personality traits and characteristics. Additionally, there are four elements—Air, Fire, Water, and Earth signs—that work together to form a comprehensive understanding of an individual's unique personality traits.

By exploring the connection between the Moon, the zodiac signs, and the elements, you can gain a deeper understanding of yourself and how these celestial influences may impact your life.

Zodiac SIGNS:

- **Aries** – March 21-April 19: Passionate, motivated, and confident leader.
- **Taurus** – April 20-May 20: Hard-headed, down-to-earth, tenacious, reliable, loyal, and sensual.
- **Gemini** – May 21-June 20: Playful and intellectually curious.
- **Cancer** – June 21-July 22: Nurturing and loyal.
- **Leo** – July 23-August 22: Comfortable being the centre of attention, drama-adoring, ambitious.
- **Virgo** – August 23-September 22: Practical and sensible.
- **Libra** – September 23-October 22: Charming, beautiful, and well-balanced.
- **Scorpio** – October 23-November 21: Extremely emotional and crave intimacy.
- **Sagittarius** – November 22-December 21: Optimistic, lovers of freedom, and hilarious.

- **Capricorn** – December 22-January 19: Overachievers, persistent, practical, and sensitive.
- **Aquarius** – January 20-February 18: Forward-thinking people who want to make the world a better place.
- **Pisces** – February 19-March 20: Artistic, deeply emotional, especially empathic, and at least a little bit psychic.

Chapter 10
Tarot Cards

Tarot cards are a tool we use to predict the future. They confirm our predictions and also provide messages from our past loved ones and angels without physically speaking. We use tarot cards to develop our intuition and psychic abilities. Oracle cards serve a similar purpose, and there is a wide range of tarot decks available for purchase, including traditional tarot decks and those featuring angels, fairies, and magical creatures. You can find tarot decks in many places, but trust your gut feeling and choose the cards that catch your eye.

A tarot deck consists of 78 cards, and while some people learn all their meanings, there are other ways to develop your skills and provide insightful and accurate readings for yourself and others. Once you have purchased your cards, focus on shuffling them and infusing them with your energy. While shuffling, think of a question or the subject you would like to know about. When you feel ready, pull a card. You can choose to deal them face down or turn them over one at a time. There are different spreads you can use for readings, but I recommend starting with a small spread of three cards. Lay them down from left to right, representing **the past, the present, and the future.**

In my experience, I did not research each individual card. Instead, I would listen to myself and understand the meaning that came to me. Look for patterns or a story in the spread. You may also become aware of different colours on the cards. Say what you see and feel, no matter how silly it may seem. Words and pictures may come to your mind as you gain more experience.

Most tarot cards come with a manual, but do what feels comfortable for you. Use your intuition throughout the process. You may even experience sensations, such as a change in temperature, or see the silhouette of your guides when using the cards. It's all about what comes directly to you. Everyone is different, so embrace that.

Chloe's top tips:

Don't panic when you see the Death or Devil card. They represent the ending of a cycle or the presence of temptation.

Remember, your Tarot cards are personal to you and carry your energy. It's important not to give them to anyone else.

Think of tarot card reading as a journey, a process of exploration and discovery.

Tarot Card Exercise:

1) Ask the person you are reading for to shuffle the cards while you mentally focus on the situation, they would like guidance on or ask them to provide a specific question.

2) Take a moment to focus on your breathing, relax, and clear your mind. Create a calm and receptive state of mind.
3) Once the cards have been shuffled, take the deck and deal three cards in a row in front of yourself, positioning them from left to right.
4) Begin to discuss what you intuitively feel the cards mean and represent. Pay attention to the symbolism, images, and emotions that arise. Share your interpretations with the person based on your understanding of the cards.
5) Explore how the interpretations connect with their past experiences and their current situation. Discuss any insights or messages that the cards may reveal about their future.

Psychic Symbols:

As you develop your psychic skills, you may begin to visualise various pictures and symbols. Understanding the meanings of these symbols can be a challenge, as there are countless images that you may encounter on your journey. Below, I have provided a few examples, but it's important to note that the significance of a symbol can vary for each individual, so it's best to describe what you see to the person you are reading for.

Keys: Symbolises problem-solving, new opportunities, or something new that involves keys.

Fish: Represents fertility or can be seen as a universal symbol of life.

Butterflies: Signifies spiritual transformation or the start of a new beginning.

Angel: Indicates a peaceful outcome and protection. Emphasises the importance of every day.

Knife: Suggests the need to cut ties or let go of something.

Moon: Connected to femininity, intuition, fertility, and emotions.

Mountains: Symbolises a quest or journey with obstacles along the way.

Rose: Represents love and can hold personal significance for the individual.

Owl: Signifies wisdom and the ability to see beyond the surface.

Police: May indicate feelings of guilt or the need to address any wrongdoing.

Tree: Encourages embracing nature and connecting with its grounding energy.

Dragonfly: Represents a carefree nature and the need for change.

Hedgehog: Symbolises child-like innocence and protection in one's life.

The Lotus: Represents awakening and spiritual growth.

Scales: Signify balance and the need for harmony in life.

Anchor: Symbolises strength, stability, and hope.

Eagle: Represents freedom and the ability to rise above challenges.

Dandelion: Symbolises healing, hope, and resilience.

Chapter 11
Manifestation

Manifestation is indeed the process of bringing something from the realm of ideas and thoughts into physical reality. It involves using our thoughts, feelings, and beliefs to attract and create the experiences, circumstances, and outcomes we desire. Visualisation is a powerful tool for manifestation, where you imagine and experience the desired outcome as if it has already happened.

While manifestation may seem far-fetched to some, many people have reported positive results from practising it consistently. By having a clear vision of what you want and aligning your thoughts, emotions, and actions with that vision, you can increase the likelihood of attracting your dreams into your life.

Here are some examples of what you can manifest:

- A new house or car: Visualise yourself living in your dream home or driving your desired car, feeling the joy and fulfilment it brings.
- A loving relationship: Imagine yourself in a loving and fulfilling relationship, experiencing the connection, support, and happiness that you desire.

- New business opportunities: Visualise yourself succeeding in your business endeavours, attracting new opportunities, clients, and financial abundance.
- Better health: See yourself in a state of optimal health, feeling energised, vibrant, and free from any physical or emotional ailments.
- More confidence: Visualise yourself being confident and self-assured in various areas of your life, whether it's public speaking, social interactions, or pursuing your goals.

Manifesting methods:

369 Method: This method involves writing down what you want to manifest three times in the morning, six times in the afternoon, and nine times in the evening. You then repeat this daily if necessary. You're holding your goal in mind throughout the day, which is helpful for tapping into your subconscious.

Journaling: One of the best places to start, no matter what you're manifesting, is journaling. By sitting with yourself every day and taking the time to journal your thoughts, you can start to recognise where you're blocking yourself and how to move forward. It really helps. While doing this, write down your goals. Another method is to write your goals on slips of paper and place them under your pillow at night.

Make a vision board: Crafting a vision board, a collage of photos, quotes, and colours representing your dreams. This helps you visualise the life you want to build for yourself. You can even hang your vision board somewhere visible in your house, setting yourself up to think about how you will manifest your dreams every time you pass by it.

Energy Exercises

Connection with your energy.

1) Sit quietly and close your eyes, focusing on your awareness outside of your body. What energy surrounds you?
2) As you inhale, imagine your energy expanding around you.
3) Take some time to do this exercise and see how large you can make your aura.
4) Do you experience anything unusual? What thoughts come to mind?
5) Keep a dated record of your experiences. What colour did you find your aura to be?

Feeling Your Energy: I find this exercise very powerful. We have smaller chakras in the palms of our hands, and this exercise will help you activate them.

1) Sit in a comfortable position with your feet flat on the floor.
2) Place your palms together and concentrate on the contact between them. You may start to feel heat building up.
3) After a few minutes, slightly separate your hands while still focusing on the same spot between your palms. Begin to slowly move your palms apart and back together, as if you are pumping air between them. You should start to feel some resistance.
4) Now gradually increase the distance between your hands with each movement, continuing the pumping action. Feel as though there is a ball of energy forming!
5) You can have fun with this ball of energy by moving your hands around and feeling its edges.

Often Asked Questions

Do you believe in Reincarnation?
It is believed that reincarnation is the process in which, upon death, the soul is believed to be reborn into a new infant or animal to live another life. The term "transmigration" refers to the passing of the soul from one body to another after death. However, I personally do not perceive this phenomenon occurring because I continue to experience communication with spirits who have passed away. If they had been reincarnated into something else, I would not be able to communicate with them in this way.

How do I connect with my loved ones? It is indeed important to trust and believe in oneself when it comes to spiritual communication. Having strong doubts can hinder the ability to connect effectively. Meditation serves as a foundational practice for enhancing communication abilities, and it helps in developing intuition and activating the third eye chakra, which is associated with higher perception and spiritual insight. Through consistent practice and self-belief, one can strengthen their connection and develop their skills in spiritual communication.

Are angels our past loved ones? No, angels are different. They are much higher up on the plane. I see angels in the form of light. We are all assigned a guardian angel from birth, and we also have other angels who provide us with love and guidance. Ask your angels to show you a sign.

If I **manifest**, will it come true? Yes, believe and anything can come true. You can manifest anything – fertility, money, love, and more.

What are Angel numbers? Angel numbers are repeating number sequences that are believed to be signs from your angels, conveying a message or providing guidance. These numbers often appear repeatedly in your life, such as on clocks, licence plates, or phone numbers. Each number holds a specific meaning and symbolism, and the combination of numbers in a sequence carries a unique message tailored to the individual receiving it. Paying attention to angel numbers and deciphering their meanings can offer insights, support, and encouragement from the spiritual realm.

Is a pendulum safe?

A pendulum is a tool we use to communicate with our guides in the comfort of our own home. Remember to ask for protection, but yes, they are safe. I would not suggest using any other tools though, for example, Ouija boards. A pendulum simply shows you physically what your energy field already knows. A Ouija board is opening a door to allow negative spirits in.

Our pets and babies in the spiritual world: Yes, our pets are still with us, just like our past loved ones, and so are our babies. If you have a termination or miscarriage, your baby will even grow in the spiritual world. How magical!

How will I see a spirit? What do they look like? All guides may appear in different ways. For example, I know Ghosts, Angels, and Spirit are different because they appear different in sight. Sometimes I may see your past loved ones in full detail, and sometimes I may just see memories directly in my mind, or they come forward and use my body as a channel – labouring my breathing, which is a sign of passing from the heart/lungs.

Empathic: Being empathic usually refers to those who understand and share the feelings and emotions of others. You simply understand how they are feeling just by looking at them.

Medium: A person who can communicate with the dead.

Psychic: Sensing things to happen before they happen.

What is a spiritual church? It is a meeting place to demonstrate healing events, mediumship circles, and more. It's looking to provide proof of the existence of spirit after death.

What is being Telepathic? The ability to send or receive thoughts, words, or images to or from another person.

Reiki: Reiki is a method of healing. It's a Japanese term meaning Universal life force energy.

How to strengthen my psychic abilities: If you look at someone and get a bad vibe for no reason, this is your psychic intuition coming through. You can practise this by meeting new people, looking beyond their appearance or how they speak, and tuning into their energy.

From Chloe:

I am grateful to each and every one of my followers during my journey of Chloe Mediumship. To my Mum and Dad, for supporting me in "being weird" and my nightmares growing up. To my partner Mason and our children, George, Charlie, and Ivy, for being there to listen and support me. And most of all, thank you to my Nan, Susan, for telling me to embrace who I am and help and support others – forever chasing rainbows. I will continue to grow and develop my skills, and so will you. Remember to trust yourself, be patient, and remember that you are reading this for a reason.

Chloe x